Heart Lines and Lyrics
....from Billy Gamble and Friends

Editors

William N. Thompson
and
Anthony J. Juliano

Illustrated by

Judi Jason

1stBooks Library
Bloomington, Indiana

This book is a work of fiction. Places, events, and situations in this story are purely fictional. Any resemblance to actual persons, living or dead, is coincidental.

© 2003 by William N. Thompson and Anthony J. Juliano.
All rights reserved.

No part of this book may be reproduced, stored in a retrieval system, or transmitted by any means, electronic, mechanical, photocopying, recording, or otherwise, without written permission from the author.

ISBN: 1-4107-3007-7 (e-book)
ISBN: 1-4107-3006-9 (Paperback)

Library of Congress Control Number: 2003092488

This book is printed on acid free paper.

Printed in the United States of America
Bloomington, IN

1st Books - rev. 06/27/03

Preface

Billy Gamble enjoyed rhymes when he was a small child. But as he grew up (or tried to grow up), he learned that he should cast away (or try to cast away) his childish ways. He went to school. In kindergarten and grade school he recited nursery rhymes. It was fun. But later in his high school and his college literature courses he learned that "poetry" just simply does not rhyme. He was confronted with a knowledge that "true poets" use words that people like Billy Gamble cannot understand or comprehend. And the words somehow didn't rhyme. Poetry was no longer fun. It was confusing, not enjoyable. It was "work." Somehow Billy Gamble "faked" his way through his English courses. He received passing grades even though he was often not able to follow the lectures or the reading assignments from the first to the last day of classes. Maybe other students felt the same. He has to think many did, although they never confessed it to him. But as he was exercising deception and moving toward his high school diploma and his three college degrees, "Doctor" Billy Gamble found a refuge of sorts in country music lyrics and tunes. There he found the fun of childish rhymes once again.

But alas, again he found that his Sisyphean mountain journey through life—in the eyes of many of his academic colleagues—was not supposed to be fun. These colleagues looked with an utter disdain upon country music much as his English professors had held for rhymes, that is, at least for rhymes that could be understood. But nevertheless, in the mode of a Sisyphean creature searching for new pathways onward and upward, be they futile or bountiful ones, Billy Gamble persisted. He even found friends and colleagues who also liked lyrics and simple rhymes. Although it was a peer group requirement that all persons between ages 8 and 30 look down their noses in disgust at country music, he was even able to find friends who actually liked this genre of music.

Billy Gamble was not alone. In fact, he and two of his friends even ventured to write some lyrics and tunes and take them to Nashville in the search for fame and fortune. Alas, the desire for sustenance and some modicum of self esteem, took him and his friends back to other day to day pursuits. But the love of lyrics and the excitement of writing simple rhymes with simple words and tunes—the essence of the traditional country music genre—has persisted. Now over 30, at least two times—he moves boldly forward in pathways he walked long ago. In his Heartlines and Lyrics, Billy Gamble unapologetically, brings together many of his simple rhymes and song words along with those he also wrote with his friends.

Like the rest of us, Billy Gamble's journey has been an uphill one often burdened by large boulders on his shoulders. But climb on he has, and climb on he does, as he often pauses to take the medicine that cures the urge to stop—he takes the medicine of celebration. The Sisyphean struggle is bearable for many only if they can infuse a healthy and close-to-excessive dose of celebration into their rock bearing travails. Heartlines and Lyrics represents a source of celebration for Billy Gamble's journey with his friends.

Billy Gamble's Friends: The Editors' Note

The editors (and primary authors) of the lyrics and heart lines below are William N. Thompson and Anthony J. Juliano. They have been friends since they met in Dr. Rutkowski's Fundamentals of Education 301 class at Michigan State University in East Lansing. That was in 1959. They soon began putting lyrics together, lyrics about life and love and other such things that concern young men in their 20s and 30s and 40s and 50s and 60s. William knows that a Kiss begins with Kay, Kay has been his wife for 38 years. They have three children Tim, Steve, Laura. Their lives together have most often found them around schools, now in Las Vegas. William teaches at the University of Nevada, Las Vegas, and Kay is a school counselor with the Clark County School District.

Anthony J. Juliano said "Oh Linda, I guess it happens to us all," way back in the 1960s. He also expressed his feelings for Linda when he penned "Thoughts of You." Tony and Linda have been together since December 1965. Tony has gone through a variety of careers inside and outside of government work. In the 1980s he owned a business consulting company. He now serves as a Dean at the Community College in Lansing. Linda is also a school counselor. There is something appropriate here, as both Bill and Tony admit to the need to be watched over by ones who have "special" training. Kay and Bill, Tony and Linda all shared undergraduate college days at M.S.U. in the early 1960s, receiving their first college degrees on the banks of the Red Cedar.

Others from those early days and days decades later have also contributed to this collection. Ted Hull also shared experiences in educational classes at M.S.U. He worked with Bill and Tony on several songs which they took to publishing houses in Nashville. Ted received his degree in special education for the visually-handicapped. One day Ted received a call from the State School for the Blind across town. The principal had heard that Ted was interested in music. Ted was asked if he would be available to be a special tutor to one of their students who wished to leave school and go on a world tour. The student was Stevie

Wonder. Stevie recorded several of the songs Ted worked on, including "Purple Raindrops," which we have included here as it was originally written. We also include some other earlier efforts that we composed as a group. Our friend Gordon Steinhauer from those early days helped with "Tonight I Shall Dream."

There are several latter day contributors. Steve Thompson grew up loving the guitar. Over the years he has put together several garage bands, and other musical groups that have performed at places such as the Great Basin Mini Brewery in Reno, Nevada, and the Cafe Roma in Las Vegas. Steve is now a music teacher in Creswell, Oregon. His friend Joshua Reisman is an attorney in Las Vegas, and Rob Pevitts is in New York City pursuing theater interests. Their "Midwest Memories" is included in this collection.

Bradley Kenny completed law school in New Orleans and now has a practice in Las Vegas. His desire for the lifestyle near the St. Charles street cars is reflected in his "Conversations with Myself," and "Carnival Tiger." Brad coauthored 1st Books Library's Over the Top: Solutions to the Sisyphus Dilemmas of Life (1st Books Library, 2003) with editor William Thompson.

The contributions from William Thompson and Anthony Juliano (most written together but some individually) are not individually marked with authorships. However those written along with Ted Hull and Gordon are marked "With Ted," or "With Ted and Gordon." The songs and lines by Brad and Steve, Josh, and Rob are indicated by their names below the lyrics.

In addition to our friends who have contributed their work to this collection, we wish to offer our special words of appreciation to Judi Jason for her original drawings. Judi is a graduate student and teaching assistant in the Communications program at the University of Nevada, Las Vegas. Judi also contributed lines to "At a Place Called Together." Special thanks are also due to Bob Potts and Mary Riddel of the Center for Business and Economic research at U.N.L.V. for their critical help in processing graphics for the volume. Dr. Janice Reid, an English Professor at the Community College of Southern Nevada did read the "lyrics" and offered critical advice that does give confidence to the editors that this effort does have "some" legitimacy in the realm of "poetry. " Additionally we offer thanks to many named and unnamed sources of inspiration for the lines in this book.

This is Anthony Juliano's first book, and William N. Thompson's third book with 1stBooks Library. He coauthored <u>Over the Top</u> with Bradley Kenny, and also wrote <u>Parables from (a Not Quite) Paradise, NV 89154</u>.

The editors also thank the staff of 1stBooks Library for their many hours of labor assembling and giving order to this volume, especially Lucy Watters and Vid Beldavs.

Heart Lines and Lyrics

And I Had it All

I Wanted a rose to grow in the snow
Rainbows forever to be in the sky
I Wanted hunger to end so all would know laughter
And never more would a small child cry

I Wanted to be master over every domain
To have the whole world at my beckoned call
I Wanted and Wanted so very very much
Then I met you and I had it all

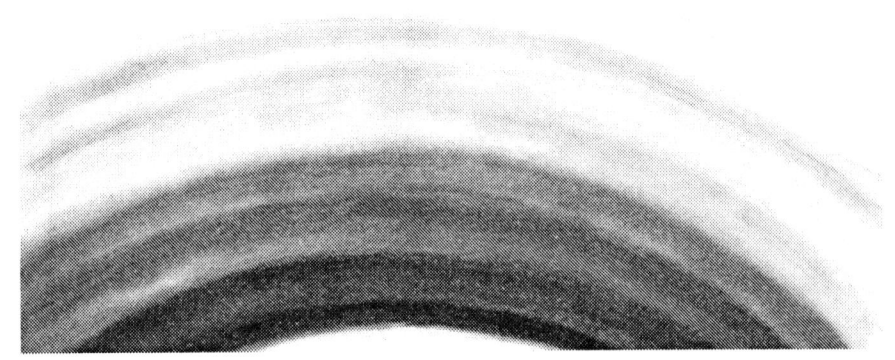

Tell Me

Tell me to finish what never began
And tell me it never can be
Tell me over and over
But I won't understand
And I won't give up the sweet memory

Tell me the feelings were gone
By the dawn's early mist
That I must get control of myself
That we never shared sweet moments of bliss
And I should write poems about someone else

Then go tell the rainbow its colors are gone
Tell the four winds that they must be still
Tell the sands of the desert
There's no more sun
If they listen, then maybe I will

And tell the raindrops to go back to the sky
Tell the skies they can never be blue
Tell all the blue birds they can no longer fly
And then tell me
To stop dreamin' of you

4

What Will Become of A Broken Heart

What will become of a broken heart
That a lovely woman is tearing apart
She'll never know how much I love her
Falling in love is so far above her
I'll never hold her
Sharing her kiss
We will never know
Those sweet moments of bliss
I've tried so hard to forget about her
But now I know I can't live without her
My world it's a shambles
Falling apart
What will become of my broken heart

What will become of a lonely life
Where the pains and heartaches stab like a knife
How can I hide this bitter feeling
And all these sad tears my heart's concealing
My world it's a shambles
Falling apart
What will become of my broken heart

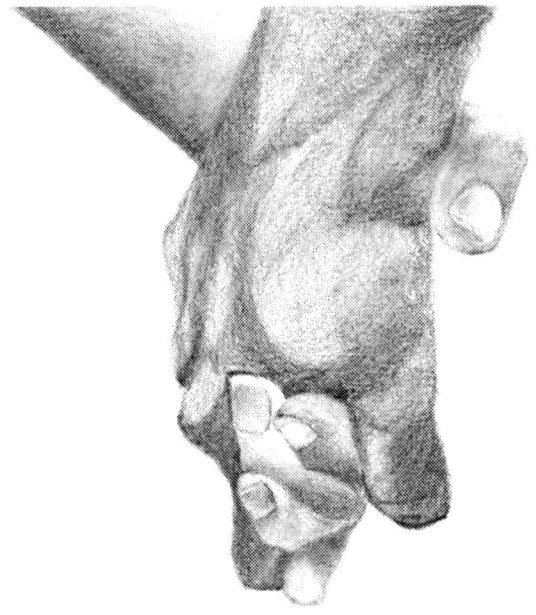

Just

Just want to go walking
Holding hands, talking
A chance to share
Precious moments of Time

Don't need any action
No fatal attractions
Just want your two eyes
To look into mine

Beginnings

A kiss
Unemotional
No Bliss
Uncontrollable
But Feelings
Reliable
Come From the Heart

Memories Intangible
Leave Questions
Unanswerable
But Desires
Undeniable
Ask
How can we start

Illusions

It never really happened girl
You've gotta understand
We never walked in moonlight
Arm in arm, hand in hand

I never held you closely
And our lips never met
It never really happened girl
So tell me, why can't I forget

Can brief moments last forever
Even if they were in dreams
Can illusions be reality
Cause that's the way it seems

I never held your heart or soul
Yet somehow I can't let go
It never really happened girl
But still I love you so

The Gambler

Pick a card, any card
The choice is yours to make
A one eyed jack, seven or nine
Ace, king, queen or eight

Pick a card, you select
Heart, diamond, club, or spade
Together for now or if you wish
Feelings that never will fade

Pick a card, if you don't like it
Go ahead and draw again
The card will be your link to me
Your real ace, your heart, your ten

Let's both pick cards together
We will make a winning hand
All faces, diamonds and aces
I'll be the king at your command

Pick a card, then make a bid
And play a no trump lead
We'll convert on all the tricks
Answering each others needs

But existence is not a card game
Not tea leaves, stars or lucky charms
Our lifeline is not upon our hands
But within each others arms

So pick a card, any card
If it's an ace or a lowly two
The cards all really mean the same
They say I'm dreaming, just waiting for you

12

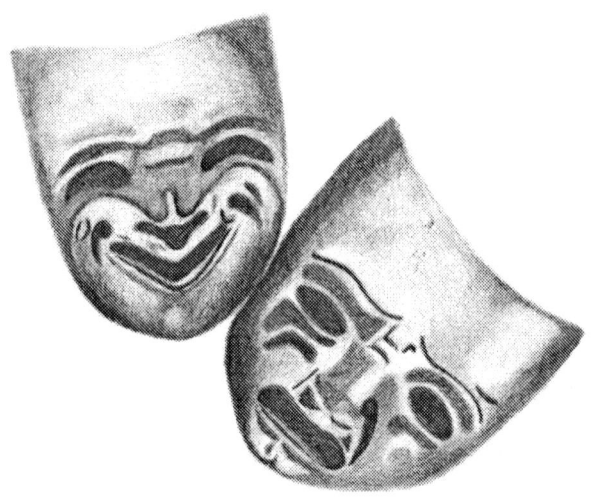

My Moods

I wonder what mood Honey's in today
Are her skies blue or are they cloudy gray
Does she wear a smile upon her face
Or does she have a frown
Is Honey's disposition up or down

I wonder what mood Honey's in today
Oh how I wish she'd throw a smile my way
If she would then I could feel Oh so good again
Cause doncha know
Honey controls the mood I'm in

14

Philosophical

A tree falls in an empty forest
But does it make a sound
A love exists yet paths don't cross
Will that love be found

To long for someone to lead me down paths
Where no one can be led
To wait for messages with words
That must be left unsaid

To try to understand and learn
What no one knows to teach
To grasp and hold onto those things
That seem just out of reach

The quest, the journey, the odyssey
Is but a search for what is true
So my mind can know, as my heart feels
That the answers lie with you

16

The Free Things in Life are Best

A hummingbird
A colored butterfly
Flowers in the desert
A clear blue sky
Morning on a hillside
Sunsets by the sea
Tulips and roses
The falling of leaves
With diamonds and gold
We might not be blessed
But we know the free things
In this life are best

The Christmas season
With trimming of trees
A sunrise at Easter
A friend's birthday
Waves on a lake
A bird in its nest
The joy of your smile
The thrill of a kiss
For castles and kingdoms
Let others contest
The free things in life
We know they are the best

Like a clear mountain stream
And an eagle in flight
A rainbow in spring
And a warm summer's night
The fireflies glow
And toes in the sand
A fresh fallen snow
The touch of your hand
Yes the free things in life
They outshine all the rest
You are my friend
And that makes life best

Worry, Wonder, and Walk

I worry about her
Where can she be
Worry about her
Does she still love me
But why do I worry
Bout a girl I once knew
I worry because I'm so blue

I Wonder about her
Where has she gone
Wonder what happened
Where did we go wrong
But why do I wonder
When I know we're through
I wonder because I'm so blue

I walk through a city
Each lonely night
People all watch me
They know I'm not right
But why am I walking
These dark steps all night through
I'm walking because I'm so blue

Existential

I want to be the one to hold your hand
I want to be the one you call your man
Oh honey can't you see
I just want to be

I want to be the one you hold real tight
I want to be the one you kiss good night
Oh honey can't you see
I just want to be

And I want to be your valentine
I want to be 'cause you're so fine
I want to be the heart you own
I want to be 'cause you turn me on

I want to be set on my heels a reelin'
I want to be filled with that lovin' feelin'
O honey can't you see
I just want to be

You're Too Good to Miss Me

Now you're too good to miss me
But you weren't too good to kiss me
Just a short while ago
You're too good to think of me
But you weren't too good to love me
Just a short while ago

So what am I supposed to do now
You've left me here so blue now
When you walked out on me I nearly cried
Can't you come back to me today now
Back into my arms to stay now
Why can't you forget all of that foolish pride

Oh you know how much I need you
So on bended knees I plead to you
Please come on back to me
I'll be right here a dreamin' of you
And you know how much I love you
So please come on back to me

Thoughts of You

I think about you when I'm happy
You're on my mind everyday
Beauty and truth, sunshine and love
I always think of you this way

I think about you when I'm weary
I need your love when I'm blue
When I need strength to carry on
These are the times I think of you

The golden sunrise sparkles the dew
A balmy breeze whispers your name
Each little bluebird sings about you
I see your teardrops in the rain

The earth as it speeds through the heavens
The moon as it dips to the sea
A falling star, a growing tree
You're in these thoughts and memories

A burning desert beckons to me
You may be on the other side
Lights of a city seen from the sea
Bring me the love within your eyes

I think about you when you're with me
You're in my dreams when you're gone
You'll always be, a part of me
Locked in my heart where you belong

You Made Me A Poet

I only offered some silly words
I only made some simple rhymes
But you've given them their meaning
You've made poetry from my lines

I only sang you some lyrics
Some tunes with foolish poems
But you've given them their melodies
And made me a singer of love songs

Reaching to others is a quest
A reason to live a reason to be
The joy of my existence answered
Your happiness my truest glee

Life's brief moments shared together
Hands held and eyes fixed to eyes
Your cheerful smile and laughter
Could I have won a greater prize

You've stood beside me and listened
Songs I've sung and you have heard
I am so love-filled and so grateful
That you have let me share my words

If you only Knew

If you only knew
What I'm going through
You wouldn't play around the way you do
If you only could see
What you're doing to me
You wouldn't break my heart the way you do

My love is yours for the asking
You know my heart belongs to you
You're just playing a game
You don't want my name
But yet you'll keep my heart won't set it free
I just got to be sure
I can't stand any more
You've got to love me now or let me be

My heart is yours for the asking
You know my love belongs to you
If you only knew
What I'm going through
You wouldn't play around the way you do
If you only could see
What you're doing to me
You wouldn't break my heart the way you do

(With Ted)

Conversations With Myself—Down the Road

Remember the Mardi Gras
I thought that I'd get sick
But I didn't

Remember Summer days in Audubon Park
The days we thought would last forever
But they didn't

Do you remember the first streetcar ride
I thought I'd get back in time
But I didn't

Remember races at the fairgrounds
I thought I'd win a million
But I didn't

Remember drinking that first jello shot
I thought I'd pass out
But I didn't

Oh I remember the time at Pat O'Briens'
I tried to put out the fire in the fountain
But I didn't

Remember looking for the House of the Rising Sun
I thought I could find it
But I didn't

Remember the Mansions along St. Charles
I thought I'd buy one
But I didn't

Remember the magic moments called New Orleans
I thought you'd come back up North
But you didn't

(Brad)

26

Does Anyone Know What Time It Is

Every hour on the hour
It's true that I don't think about her
Everyday about this time
I never let her cross my mind

Safely hidden is her memory
It cannot escape its hideaway
My minds forgotten we are apart
If my mind could only tell my heart

For there it is she waits she waits
I can't leave, she can't escape
Forsaken dreams in a prison home
Deeply locked within, wherever I roam

With me each hour, on the hour
As the mind denies the thought about her
Lost love the heart still seeks to find
But I never let her cross my mind

Missing You

A day without music
No melody and no words
A day without smiles
No laughter is heard

No raindrops no rainbows
No silver linings in blue
No stars in the heavens
It's a day without you

At a Place Called Together

At a place we call together
Two hearts beat on as one
At a time that's called forever
You'll be right here in my arms

Beneath the snow capped peaks
Of purple mountains ever grand
By enormous white capped waves
Crashing into sundrenched sands

On the pathways through the forests
With majestic redwood trees
Across meadows filled with wildflowers
In a warmest summer's breeze

Nature's grace will link our two hearts
At a time that's called forever
As we grasp onto one another
At a place we call together

(With Judi)

Twice a Day

If only once in a while I could be right
I would choose to be right in your arms
Stars and clear skies would keep me on course
Each day I'd hold to your charms

If I could be right, right there by your side
How could happy be some other way
If I could just be like a broken down clock
If I could only be right twice a day

I'm Going to Disneyland

The hour was bright
The day promised sunshine
So we gathered with hurry and glee
There was Huey, Looie, Dewey
Donald Duck and Goofy
And the Bear Country Jamboree

We all came together
For some pickin' and singing
For laughs and good feelings to share
But clouds came on the horizon
As we soon discovered
It was a just a Mickey Mouse Affair

Now a heart needs sunshine
For a heart to love
I found brightness and radiance in her smile
I entrusted my feelings
To her tender care
But it lasted such a short while

The more my desires
The less her concerns
No holding hands, no kisses to share
I cried out in vain
But alas all for naught
It was a Mickey Mouse Affair

Tonight I Shall Dream

Tonight I shall dream
I'll dream of a valley
Where cool breezes blow
Ever so gently

With honeysuckles everywhere
Their fragrant perfumes fill the air
And the babbling brooks are playing there
And you wait for me

Tonight I shall dream
Of pine scented flowers
Where the sun turns the snow
Into fountains of pearls

Tonight I shall walk
Through the meadows of flowers
A hint of true bliss
Will linger for hours

I'll pick from the trees
The fruit of this valley
I'll drink from its spring
The clear crystal waters

The deep glowing moon
Will return me to slumber
Where the cool breezes call
You are waiting for me

(With Ted and Gordon)

Freud

I never thought
I was crazy
Paranoid, schizoid,
Or catatonic

But honey you drove me
Up the wall
When you said
It had to be platonic

Daydreaming

I dare not get the wrong idea
If she smiles at me today
Cause she might be a happy person
Cause that just might be her way

I dare not get the wrong idea
If she brushes my arm with her hand
And says I remind her of a movie star
I just dare not misunderstand

I dare not get the wrong idea
If her lips touch mine in a gentle kiss
And she says she likes my nearness
Moments of closeness just like this

I dare not get the wrong idea
If she moves softly into my arms
And tells me that she loves me
That she's been captured by my charms

No I guess I dare not get the wrong idea
Just cause she smiled at me today
Cause you know she's a very happy person
And I guess that's just her way

Butterflies in a Backyard

Butterflies cannot thrive without gardens
Gardens need loving care to grow
Butterflies are illusions outside closed windows
We must go where the butterflies go

Venture outward let your hand nourish flowers
Make them blossom and show us the way
Butterflies will come fly beside us
And tell us our love's here to stay

Oh Linda

Oh Linda
I never thought I'd ever fall
And then I met you
I guess it happens to us all

At first I wasn't very sure
But as the days went by I knew
Oh Linda
I guess I'm falling in love with you

I had to tell you
How very much you meant to me
And now I worry
Maybe our love will never be

How come I feel the way I do
Linda I got make you see
Linda I love you
And you're the only girl for me

42

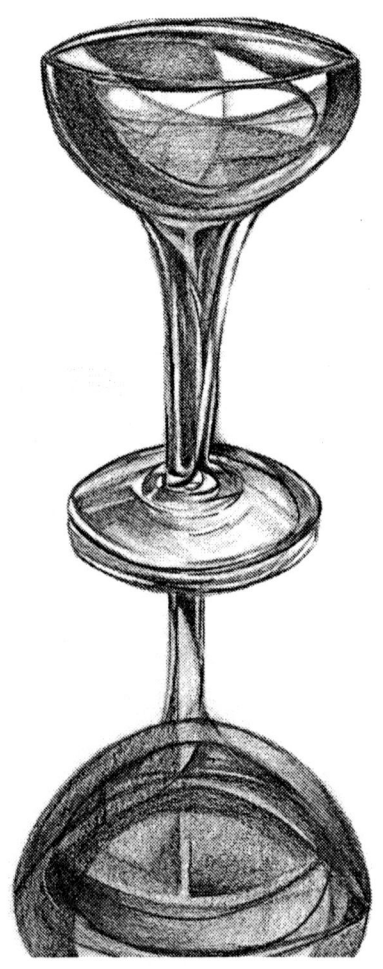

Again

Sometime to see you again
Sometime to hold you again
Sometime to kiss you again

Tonight a brew light
And a toast to a Friend
A toast to Sometime
A toast to Again

The Poor Poet

Now consider the poor poet
So silent is his verse
He has no love to share his lines with

Ah, but now think of his fate
It could even be worse
If his one love doesn't know he exists

Lonesomest Town

The streets are dark and dreary
There ain't a soul around
The bars are all deserted
A friend cannot be found
I visit all the old hangouts
The way it used to be
But nowhere does a voice call out
Bill have a drink with me

Cause it's a lonesome town
Lonesomest town in the world

A girl I knew named Sally
Once lived in this old town
She said when Uncle Sam is through with you
I'll still be around
But when I call her on the phone
A voice so loud and clear
Said Sally married your best friend
And she got out of here

Cause it's a lonesome town
The lonesomest town in the world

So here I'm walking all alone
Along these lonely streets
Thinking of the things we did
And the folks we used to meet
What is my life coming to
Why can't I settle down
I guess I'll have to pack my bags
And leave this weary town

Cause it's a lonesome town
The lonesomest town in the world

(With Ted)

Thanksgiving Prayer

Someone to listen to me
Someone to make my heart ring
Someone to call buddy and friend
Someone who wants me to sing

Someone to pick up my mail
Someone who reads my poetry
Someone who's smile makes my day complete
For that Someone I give thanks to Thee

Purple Raindrops

Purple raindrops, beautiful flowers
I daydream for hours
Since that day I met you
I cannot forget you
Oh, tell me what am I going to do

I see strange things
So many strange things
I think you have changed things
Since that day I met you
I cannot forget you
Oh, what am I going to do

I guess I'll get along
The best way that I can
Until you come back around
And take me by my hand

I hear bells ring
I hear angels sing
Oh, I know what that means
Since that day I met you
I'll never forget you
Oh! What am I going to do

(With Ted)

Are You Happy

I gave you candy, rainbows and flowers
I made you the words of my song
Are you happy that you came into my life
Are you happy that I came along?

I touched your fingers, I held your soft hand
I pressed your lips gently to mine
Are you happy that you came into my life
Are you happy that we shared the time?

I've seen the sunshine, 'cause I've seen your smile
I want dreams in your eyes to come true
I'm so happy that I came into your life
I'm so happy my trail led me to you

50

My Future has Past

Now all my dreams are memories
Sweet moments from the past
Fantasies of times gone bye
Of a time that would not last

I know heaven's not over the rainbow
In specs of stardust I can't hold
Heaven it is right here on Earth
You see, I've seen the pot of gold

Seasonal Thoughts

If it was O.K. on Saint Valentine's Day
Why have you given me up for Lent
You're an angel who glows with wings and halos
There is no doubt that you've been heaven sent

I got a most lovely card, you called me a bard
When I sang my love songs just for you
A yellow flower so sweet was my most special treat
Bright baloons colored my cloudy skies blue

As I held your hand, I felt magically grand
You said our love was here to stay
Now I feel so alone, oh tell me where have you gone
Why did you spread your wings and fly away

Cupid's Day found us close, I loved you the most
And you told me you felt the same way
If it wasn't sin then, why can't you love me again
If it was O.K. on Saint Valentine's Day

The Working Woman's Man's Blues

She gave it all at the office
It's all over everything's done
She paid her dues but he's got the blues
Nothing's there when she reaches home

She gave it all at the office
No song's left, no rhyme, there's no poem
The desire is through, she's worn out too
He stares at her and feels so alone

Someday maybe they can be together
Holding hands like when love was new
They won't give a lick, she'll just call in sick
But today there is work she must do

54

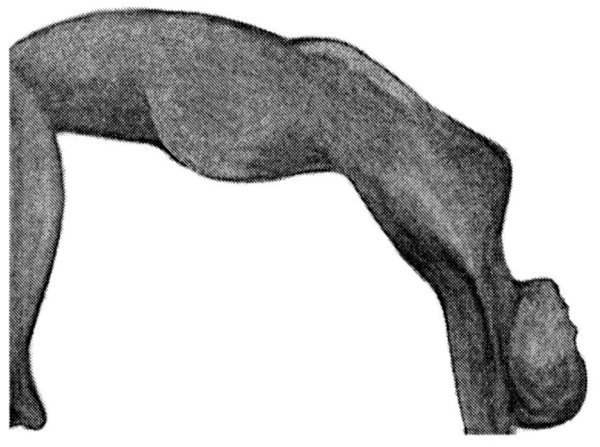

Guilt

Minutes and hours turn into days
You're with me all of my time
Deeply ingrained in my every thought
My soul's trapped with a guilty mind

Aroused feelings, senses, emotions
And dreams where we never part
Can't leave me alone can't release me
There's no freedom for my guilty heart

I know I can go to hell for my thinking
And roast eternally in hot fires of coal
So why can't I have a guilty body
Along with a guilty heart, guilty mind, guilty soul

(With Ted)

Midwest Memories

Coming home today
I'll see you there
You just may not notice me
With this gray in my hair
Cry me a river
Sing me to sleep
I've lived a long life
And I've walked a lonely street

But I cannot escape
Where it is that I am from
And I want to forget
These things that I have done
Midwest dreams have gone by
I've come back for you
I've come back to die

Hold me in your arms
Mend my city heart
I don't know why I had to go
Or why we had to part
Show me the way
I'm lost with out you
But I'll come back home
So we can start anew

But I cannot escape
Where it is that I am from
And I want to forget
These things that I have done
Midwest dreams a have gone by
I've come back for you
I've come back to die

(Josh, Steve and Rob)

May Day

Fields of flowers
Crowd springtime hillsides
But the fields I cannot see

For the prettiest flower
Is in my heart to grasp
The one rose my only need

So from a hot desert land
Grace my heart grace my hand
Let me hold a petal of delight

And encompass fragrance
As joy proclaims the presence
All memory brings moments to sight

So in the big crowd
I have but one rose to face
That carries desired smiles my way

A blessing to cling to
The full year around
Made most special this first day of May

60

Diamond Ring

I'm going to buy my girl a diamond ring
So she'll keep me on her mind
I'm going to buy my girl the biggest ring in town
Then she'll know she belongs to me

Cause a good woman among all the rest
Is sometimes kind a hard to find
I'm going to buy my girl a diamond ring
So she'll keep me on her mind

When I own anything I paint it up
And the boys they'll know it belongs to me
I'm going to buy my girl the biggest ring in town
Then they'll know that she's mine

When they see her coming down the street
My how that diamond's going to shine
I'm going to buy my girl a diamond ring
So she'll keep me on her mind

An Affair of the Heart

An affair of the heart
Spirits entwined
Special moments together
A meeting of minds

Eternally sharing
What the ages can't part
Hands softly touching
An affair of the heart

Carnival Tiger

He told me the tale
Of the Carnival Beast
A mean-spirited tiger
With flesh for its feast

I was so boyish
Childlike and such
So I heeded all warnings
And I did not sleep very much

So the fateful day came
Yes the day finally arrived
A Tuesday in February
I wondered could I survive

That day I met the tiger
Just two of us one on one
A masked beast he was
Ah yes, the fight had begun

I demanded him to throw
All his plastic pleasures
Then I'd haul them all in
And I'd barter for pleasures

I now know the Carnival Tiger
I know that I fought a good fight
Now I wait three sixty five more
For another Mardi Gras night

(Brad)

I've got my pride

Why can't I beg her on bended knees
Why must a man always stand tall
Is a man full of so much lonely
Really better than the man who crawls

But I've got my pride
I've got my pride
When the nights are cold
And there's no one to hold
I've got my pride

The coward dies a thousand deaths
The real man one time only
The man accepts what fate hands out
The coward begs to not be lonely

The winter's bleak the clouds roll in
The chill tears right to the bone
The coward shares warmth of scornful arms
While I freeze in my castle alone

Until the Twelfth of Never...

My fantasy shall be my valentine
My hope she's in these arms of mine
My desire a time not far away
My wish we'll share that treasured day
My yearn her eyes for me to see
My want is that she be close to me
Until the twelfth of never....such a long long time
My fantasy shall be my valentine

The Past, The Present, The Future

Five months ago I kissed her
Five months ago Today
Five months ago I kissed honey
Oh how fast time does slip away

I dream of a wonderful future
A beautiful time when again I'll say
Five months ago I kissed honey
It was five months ago today

(With Brad)

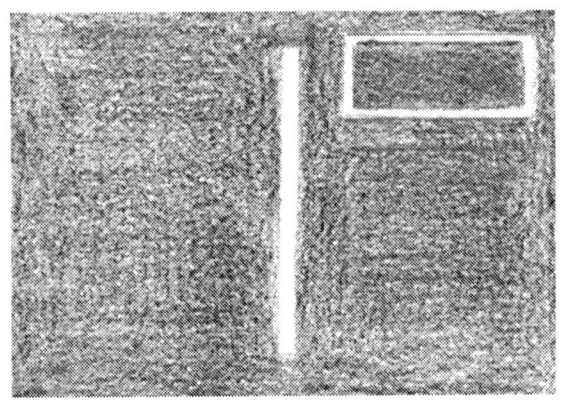

The Blue Picture Post Card

You sent me a blue post card
A blue picture post card
It told me good bye
No reason why
It had to be
Yes it was a blue post card
A going away card
It left me blue for without you
There's nothing for me
Oh where could you be

That little message
Nearly broke my poor heart
Cause that little message
It put us miles apart
Yes it was a sad greeting
Left my poor heart bleeding
Oh why must I grieve
Oh why did you leave
And where did you go
Oh please let me know

There's only tears for me
Since you're not around
This once happy city
Is like that lonesome town
Since I got that blue post card
Good bye and don't wait card
Will still be friends
If we meet again
Somewhere someday
I'm going away

(With Ted)

A Holiday Thought From Acts 20:35

Be so thankful that we can be giving
That we have more than we'll ever need
That we've been called upon to help others
We've been called on to deliver good deeds

It is so true we are blessed to be givers
You give warm smiles to all that you meet
The thought of you gives me cheer all through the year
Your friendship my thanksgiving treat

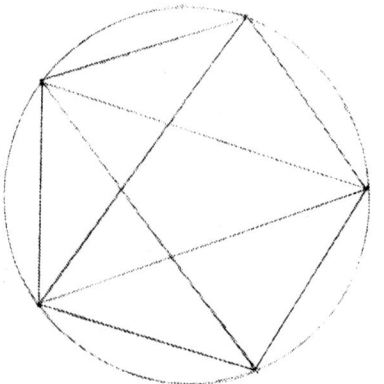

Isosceles Triangles

I realized a tragic thing was happenin'
For a triangle of love had swiftly grown
I felt our future slipping through my fingers
From a happy growing love your heart had flown

You've got a crush on my best friend
What's going to happen
Where will it end
I know that I will end up blue
I'll lose your love his friendship too

You hold me and you tell me that you love me
But your kisses and your eyes say its a lie
I feel the pains of loneliness inside me
For a love and a friendship soon may die

(With Ted)

The Other Guy

The other guy is always handsome
The other guy has all the charms
And while I'm holding her in my dreams
The other guy's got her in his arms

All I Can Do

All I can do
Is look at you
But my heart thinks
Of romance

If I were free
Would you look at me
Could you give
My heart a chance

(With Ted)

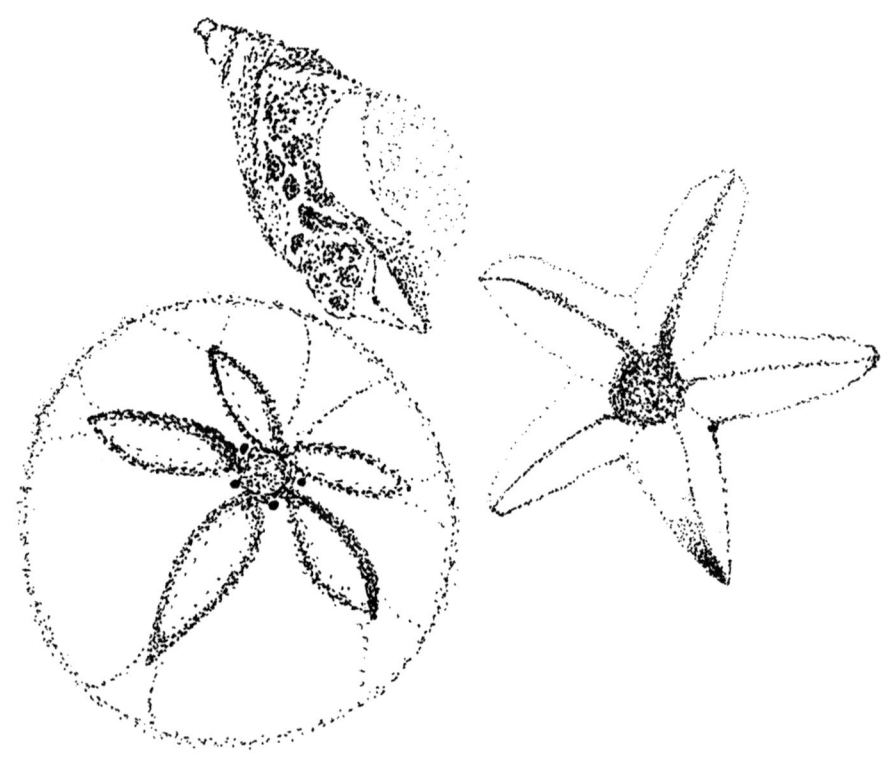

Perspectives

Together but for a few moments
Eyes meeting and talking that's all
A small space shared in a lifetime
Where other people and duty must call

A small space remembered midst turmoil
Of tasks and so much work to get done
Together but for a few moments
'Tis fate with our lives on the run

I know there must be greater powers
A good God who could grant me more time
To see your face to look again in your eyes
To have you near this heart of mine

So today I went to my church service
Knowing what counts above everything else
I prayed that God would give peace to the world
That's important—I'll take care of myself

(With Ted)

Under the Spell of Evil

Met her in a tavern
Just a honky tonk place
I knew in a moment
One look in her face
That she was the devil
But I saw angel wings
And when I should have been crying
I heard my heart sing

I belonged to another
And it just wasn't right
For us to steal off together
In the darkness of night
But I'd have gone to hell
For the heaven she'd give
I knew Evil spelled backwards was live

Evil spelled backwards is L-I-V-E
Her love was sweet poison
But I crave and I need
When she held me closely
I knew it just couldn't be
But Evil spelled backwards is
L-I-V-E

Can there really be life
If you play the game straight
Not to stray from the one
You've been given by fate
Denying the passions
You want to achieve
Told always to suffer
Be silent, believe

Then she came along
And brought that old world down
Like humpty dumpty
Broken there on the ground
I heard the voice of sin
Calling out to me "give"
I knew Evil spelled backwards was live

E-V-I-L, I know that it's sin
But when were together
I'm livin' again
When I hold her closely
I know it just shouldn't be
But Evil spelled backwards is L-I-V-E

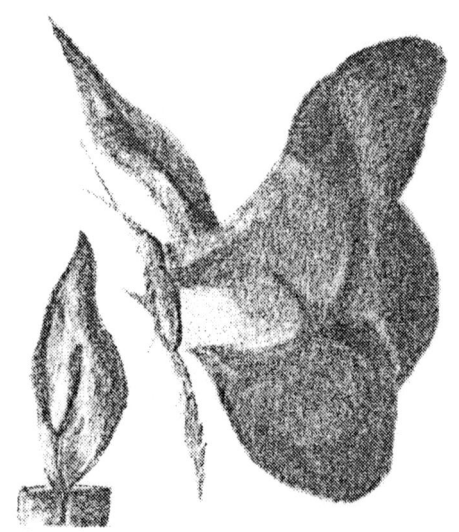

Thanatos

I know your love would destroy me
So why do I call out your name
Ah! Why do the lemmings march to the sea
Why's the moth drawn to a flame?

A Spray of Hearts

A spray of hearts should fall at your feet
And be scattered all about the ground
So when perchance you should take a pause
You'll know that love's all around

For it surrounds you at every moment
No matter the place no matter where
In flowers, in snowflakes in sunshine or rain
And when you feel love you'll know that I'm near

Infatuation

It makes me feel good, so warm and happy
Can I keep it from bothering my soul
How can I deal with infatuation
To make sure it's kept under control

I'm fully content just having you near me
But in my dreams I'm never quite sure
Can infatuation exist with just a smile and a glance
Need its nurturing demand something more

Perhaps we can reserve it just for special moments
And not push it hard day after day
Is there anything we can do with infatuation
So we can keep it from going away

So where are the answers, are they in your eyes
Or with intuition that's sent from above
Tell me what can I do with infatuation
To keep it from turning to love

(With Brad)

Caducous

Autumn leaves reveal true splendor
Red, orange, yellow, the brilliant glow
The world is showing its special beauty
Just before their final fall

Once green an infant in its budding
With fresh life to greet the spring
We wondered what we would call it
It seemed that it was just a fling

It persisted as summer brought forth fruit
To nourish to foster to share
Heat pressed upon the long long days
It grew and we called it affair

Next followed fall splendor and color
As we first sensed that all could end
Might rare beauty be cast into ashes
We needed a word, and we said friend

Then trees in the cold, bald and empty
Branches greeted by snow from above
The seasons have turned and yet all remains
In winter we understood love

In winter all is but sleeping
The reality is life's true fantasy
No fling no affair no friendship
Love endures-thank God for memories

Heart, Soul, and Love

I see your heart in the clear blue sky
In a deep red rose, in the mountains high
In a maple leaf, in a snow filled pine
Your heart I see it's in my valentine

I know your soul it's in each happy face
I see in a crowd wherever the place
In all my poems in each and every rhyme
Your soul I know it's in my valentine

I feel your love in the gentle breeze
Moving through the forest coming off the seas
In your precious voice as you speak a line
Your love I feel it's in my valentine

It is a priceless gift given to everyone
Your footsteps on my planet third from the Sun
God's most special gift given for humankind
Your heart soul your love it's in my valentine

October 31

Winds of truth blow cold, leaves fall from trees. Yellow, red, pale brown, orange. Softly impaling frosted ground. Sunshine fades, summer is gone, fall is departing. An admission. Winter has to be.

The night of reckoning arrives. A moment when we can no longer fool reality. For just one night, for but a fleeting speck of time, we must venture out into the cold. To grasp the truth, to face it, to let it face us. We must look at the world as it really is, look at others as they really are, let others looks at us. We put aside all make-up, hair-styles, convention and cover—tools that only conceal. We stop playing games, we stop filling roles. No more masquerade, now only the truth. We are trapped with the truth. We may struggle against it, but we do so in vain. So we surrender. We open our eyes. We take off our costumed coats, we remove the false paint from our eyes, off our faces, and the dye comes out of our hair.

We venture out into the night, into the cold, just as we really are, accepting the truth, about ourselves, about others. We set aside the styles that only conceal, the pretenses that only fool. We play no games. There are no roles to play, no butcher, baker, candlestick maker, no policeman, no chief, no Indian, no father, son, mother, daughter, teacher, student, husband, wife. Only people. Only people, as we really are.

My neighbor appears as he really is, a pirate. Another is a tiger, his true identity. His wife Darth Vader, a friend is a weasel, another is truly a princess, and a rabbit appears, and a bear, a cinderella, a chipmunk. And we are there. And we are beggars. Yet we do not retreat in shame. We admit to what we are. And we allow ourselves to have feelings. We choose the right words. They are honest words. We look at each other. We say "love." And in the cold night of honesty, we find a special warmth. We beg, and we are given sweetness. We feel blessed as we receive. Then….

We return to warm houses. We isolate ourselves from that world. It becomes distant. We hide in corners and we start counting our possessions, our candy. We grab for our masks and costumes of deceit, and we put them on again. We forget our feelings. We deny that we said "love." We deny the truth. We take on roles. We play games. We are hidden from others, we have hidden from ourselves. We pretend it did not happen. We say it will never happen again. But....

On another cold evening, as another fall approaches another winter, for but a fleeting speck of time, it will happen. Again. Our Brigadoon. Our Halloween.

Candles Mean Warmth and Light

One more candle its flame shall burn
To celebrate your special day
To shine upon each stepping stone
Taken on your journey's way

One more candle its flame shall burn
Making pathways for all much brighter
To burn to honor the helping hand
Making burdens of others much lighter

One more candle its flame shall burn
For struggles over so many a mile
Now have your candle and cake and eat it too
You deserve it, now give yourself a smile

94

Christmas. Christmas!

Will I cross your mind at Christmas time
Midst all the joy and yuletide pleasures
Just a thought among the gifts unwrapped
Counted with the moment's treasures

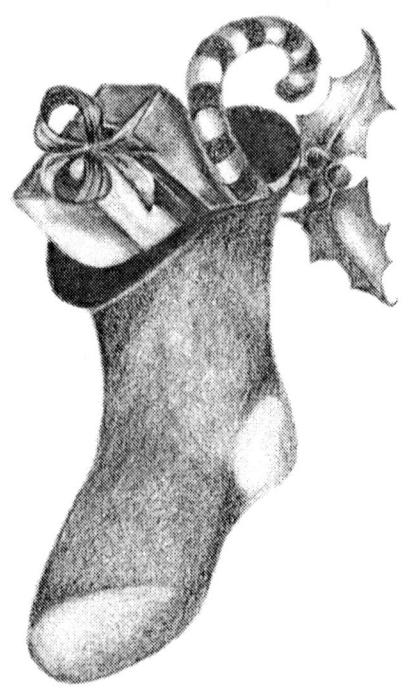

A Christmas Stocking

A Christmas stocking to hang with joy
Midst the lights the tinsel and greens
To be filled with those hopes and wishes
That can be brought forth from all our dreams

A Christmas stocking to hang with glee
On that path of so many many miles
That started a journey down a memory lane
That's been filled with laughter and smiles

A Christmas stocking to hang with cheer
And with the thoughts that bring delight
Of the season, of friendship, and of love
Thoughts that make the heart feel so light

The Christmas stocking to hang so near
That it might fit over the most precious toe
Of one who gives me joy glee and cheer
One who makes my whole existence to glow

A Gift from a Magi?

What can I give this girl
Who has everything she needs?
Her days are filled with laughter
Her laugh so filled with glee

She knows no nights of lonely
Her heart it knows not pain
To make her life complete now
Not a single thing remains

Could I give to her green emeralds
The finest silk and sweet perfume
Could I take her to Jamaica
Could I fly her to the moon

She's been there and she's done that
For her to want more would be greed
This girl who has everything
This girl who needs not me

So ponder must I the question
For the Answer holds my fate
All I will do is give her my love
Cause she has keys to heaven's gate

"We Shall Not Repeat This Mistake"

Peace Memorial at Hiroshima

We Shall Not Repeat This Mistake
The sign proclaims so plain to see
But tell me just who is this we
Is it them, or is it you and Me?

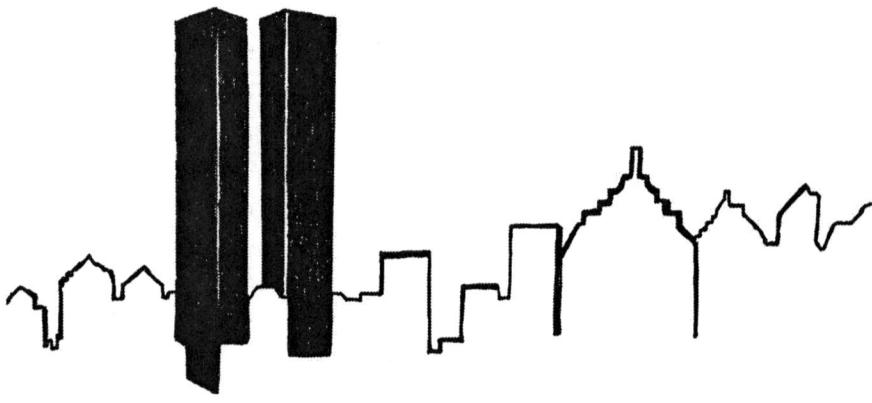

I Tried to Write a Poem

I tried to write a poem
While I was flying on a plane
I tried to write a poem
When I got out and walked in rain
I tried to write a poem
But things could never ever be the same
I just wanted to say I love you

I tried to write a poem
In a car as I drove away
I tried to write a poem
But darkness covered up my way
I tried to write a poem
The words I could not find nor say
I just wanted to say I love you

I tried to write a poem
My mind was twisted full of doubts
I tried to write a poem
There was not joy nor happy shouts
I tried to write a poem
But tell me what is this all about
I just wanted to tell you I love you

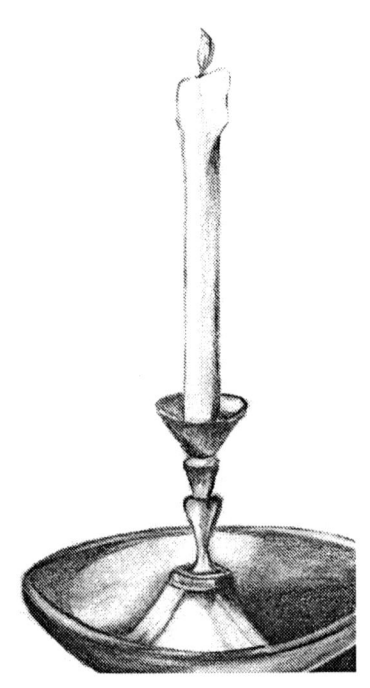

By Walls and Fences

Candles cards and flowers
Placed up beside the wall
By ordinary common people
Who don't understand at all

Candle flames burning eternal
Bringing light allowing day
Delivering us through darkness
Guiding our paths onto His way

Cards their caring words recite
Messages from so many hearts
Saying their journey's not over
Their real journey it only starts

For whom the candle burns
The cards call out in vain
Flowers can't cover hopelessness
As petals scatter in the rain

Why him, why her, why them
We can't know it isn't clear
But the knowledge it too will come
As time will draw us near

Candles cards and flowers
Together in gardens full of stone
Seeking to void an emptiness
That one day we must face alone

God's Grace

All my goodness lies with friends I know
Ones who give kindness everywhere they go
Ones who stick with me whenever I am low
The one who shares joy with her special glow
All my goodness lies with friends that I know

My goodness springs from work of children's hands
From a son helping others in a far distant land
A daughter counselling poor souls to better plans
A boy giving the world music with guitar and a band
My goodness springs from work of children's hands

My goodness is reflection of things others do
Without their devotion skies could not be blue
Rivers would run backwards a moon could never be new
We'd just be lonely creatures as if caged in a zoo
My goodness is reflection of God's grace and you

CPSIA information can be obtained
at www.ICGtesting.com
Printed in the USA
FFOW02n0901250417
34937FF